MW01107615

Happy Birthday
To: Dorothy with
Prosperity

From: Mike &
Faith
Nihelcich
2-11-12

Think & Be Happy

365 Empowering Thoughts To Lift Your Spirit

Shadonna Richards, R.N.

INFINITY
PUBLISHING.COM

Copyright © 2009 by Shadonna Richards

ISBN 0-7414-5703-2

Published by:

INFINITY
PUBLISHING.COM

1094 New DeHaven Street, Suite 100
West Conshohocken, PA 19428-2713
Info@buybooksontheweb.com
www.buybooksontheweb.com
Toll-free (877) BUY BOOK
Local Phone (610) 941-9999
Fax (610) 941-9959

Printed in the United States of America

Published November 2009

This book is dedicated with love to Solomon,
the happiest person I know.
And to anyone who wants to be happy.

About the Author

Shadonna Richards is the author of *A Gift of Hope: 52 Ways to Live a Better Life.* She is additionally a motivational speaker and registered nurse who works with cancer patients. She firmly believes in the power of happiness, a skill we can all master. The former newspaper columnist is the author of more than 250 newspaper articles and inspirational stories. Her work has appeared in various publications including *The Toronto Star, Toronto Sun, Word Magazine, Scarborough Mirror* and *Metro Newspaper* with a combined readership of 2 million readers. She has a Bachelor of Arts Degree in Psychology and lives in Canada with her husband and son.

You may contact Shadonna by e-mail at shadonna@ymail.com or visit her at *www. thinkandbehappy.org or www.shadonnarichards.net* or readers are invited to join Shadonna on Facebook at *www.facebook.com/shadonna.richards* or MySpace at *www.myspace.com/shadonnarichards.*

Acknowledgments

With the deepest gratitude, I wish to thank You, God, for Your divine guidance, the gift of life, providing me the ability to write so that I can share my experiences with others and for everything I've been blessed with in my life.

Special thanks to Marielle Marne who provided the copy editorial assistance as well as valuable feedback to "Think and Be Happy."

To Yvonne Blackwood for her valuable insights and limitless support. And a special thanks to Dr. Bob Nozik, Lionel Ketchian, Irene Watson, and Catherine Pulsifer.

A very special, heartfelt thank you to Barb Joefield, Dr. Lefebrve, Dr. Wilcock, Dr. Farrington, Mike Imbery, Carolene, Dr. Cherry, Gail, Angie, Tess, Kalsi, Cynthia, Lena, Claudette, Richard and Kiki.

A very special thank you to Kim L. and staff.

To my awesome team of colleagues at the hospital, too many to name but inclusive of Linda, Ingrid, Pearlina, Lisa, Catherine, Rebecca, Amy, Deborah, Nasrin and Kim. Thanks for your continued support. And to the extraordinary patients who have touched my life in a special way by showing me the value of how precious time really is.

With much appreciation, I wish to thank the leaders, philosophers, speakers and all those whom I've quoted for their words of wisdom.

A special thank you to all the readers who helped make "A Gift of Hope" an Amazon.ca top 100 bestseller in motivational books in 2009.

And a very special heartfelt thank you to each and every member of my family and to all my friends for their continued support, wisdom and love. Too many to name but inclusive of my parents, especially my wonderful mother, Merdella, who first set me on the path to positive thinking by introducing me to *The Power of Positive Thinking* by Dr. Norman Vincent Peale. To my loving grandparents, Nesitta, Godwin, Monica and Percell. To Sean, Charmaine, Kumari,

Ashley, Nekaya, Rose, Kingsley, Irie, Ianna, Gavin, (RIP Rodney), Jasmine, Nathan, Anthony, Rashan, Paulet, Rosemary, Veline and family, Naomi and family, Jason and family, Steadly, Charles and family, Cint and family, Mr. & Mrs. Lee, Hyacinth, Marcel and family, Mrs. Ellis, Georgia, Angela, Nyle, Debbie, Tashna, (RIP Estina Whitter), Mitzie, Michelle, Fennella, Gary and family, Ingrid, Rev. Basil Miller and anyone else I did not mention.

And finally, I express my deep appreciation to my wonderful husband, Jermaine, for his unconditional love, and to our blessed son, Solomon, for lighting up our life.

Dear Reader,

Welcome to the next phase of your happiness journey—a journey about feeling good about who you are regardless of your situation. I have to be honest, over the years, I have become what you would call an "incurable optimist," but this journey has not been an easy one. Through many tribulations and challenges, I've learned that happiness is an internal resource. Thus, it is our thoughts that make our life what it is—whatever we dwell on—good or bad—becomes our life. So, I made the conscious decision to focus and direct my mental energies on healthy thoughts and positive perceptions.

Like you, I kept searching for happiness only to realize, like Dorothy in the Wizard of Oz, that what I was looking for, I had it all along. Within. That's the beauty of it all, there is so much we are capable of doing. As a teacher and a student of positive thinking/psychology, I wish to share my research from lessons learned, articles I'd written as a journalist, and in my professional experience as a nurse who works with cancer patients with you in my second book, "Think and Be Happy." This book is a collection of short, empowering messages to boost your spirit and serve as a quick reminder to make happiness your goal every day of the year.

Having studied the great thinkers of our time and earning my first degree in psychology, it only seemed like a natural progression. I've had an advantage in that my wonderful mother started me on the pathway to positive thinking as a child when she encouraged me to read Dr. Norman Vincent Peale's "The Power of Positive Thinking." Wow, what a life changing experience! I've always wondered why some who have less and experience adverse conditions can be more content and at peace within, while others who have plenty feel they could never be happy, are lacking spiritually or are waiting for something else or someone else to provide them with joy. The latter is a type of happiness that rarely lasts. It has to come from within.

We are quite capable of servicing our own lives—if only we'd give ourselves the credit. While working on this book, I couldn't help but notice a higher level of euphoria that washed over my spirit—just by focusing on research about happiness. It is true that your mood is heavily influenced by whatever you choose to focus your thoughts on. My hopes are that you will think of this book as a mini spiritual escape or mind vacation every time you read one or more entries per day.

Like most of the books on happiness, I've focused on promoting happiness from within. What makes this book unique is its bite-size information on a day to day basis. An empowering collection of uplifting thoughts, based on timeless wisdom and other resources, to sustain your spirit through each blessed day.

May you find inner-peace, relaxation and happiness as you journey through the pages of "Think and Be Happy."

Warmest regards,
Shadonna

"The joyfulness of a man prolongeth his days."
--Proverbs 10: 2

Think and Be Happy

You can be happy today. Right now. At this very moment. Regardless of your situation or any mistakes you've made. Once you believe you have the power within to choose your mood. Once you truly *want* to be happy . . . no matter what. It is your constitutional right and divine purpose in life to experience deep, lasting joy. Instead of drowning in pessimism and resentment, you can change your thinking to flow with optimism and hope. Decide to de-clutter your brain of multiple issues of the past and live completely in the blessed moment. Deep, lasting happiness comes from being satisfied within, independent of what others may think of you or how the world treats you or what possessions you have. This is the type of happiness that can never be stripped away from you when the tides change direction. Scientific studies have shown that habitually happy people have similar experiences to unhappy people. The difference being what they choose to dwell on. As legendary coach, John Wooden, once opined: "If we magnified blessings as much as we magnify disappointments, we would all be much happier." Happy people also tend to live longer, healthier and enjoy a greater quality of life. Happiness is a skill that can be taught and learned. The United States Declaration of Independence includes the importance of well-being by asserting it is an "unalienable" constitutional right. Each person has the right to "life, liberty and the pursuit of happiness." From this day forward, make it your mission to assert your right to happiness.

Happiness is a choice you make. It is not dependent on anything outside of yourself but acts independently. Choose to be content with who you are and all that you've become while you journey to becoming more.

Think and Be Happy

If you desire a slice of happiness, you must first clear off your memory plate of past hurts, disappointments and the residue of bitter memories. Refill your soul with joy and inner peace by concentrating on the favorable aspects of your life.

Groom your thoughts every now and then by trimming off doubts, washing away pessimism, polishing your mentality with optimism, styling your attitude with enthusiasm—you'll emerge more beautiful and precious than you could ever imagine.

"Where there is life, there is hope," opined Roman philosopher, Publius Terentius Afer. Once we have life, there is always a possibility for change. For new beginnings. For endless possibilities. Never, never relinquish hope.

Be open to anything. You never know what or who will bring added joy into your life. Sometimes we search in one area or for one person to find love only to realize it was at our door all along. Life is full of miracles, surprises and revelations. Jean-Antoine Petit-Senn, 18th Century French-Swiss poet, once wrote, "Happiness is where we find it, but rarely where we seek it."

Meditate on the treasures in your life that matter. Accumulating quality friendships and strong family ties is more valuable than amassing financial wealth. Love and support from favorable relationships are what truly enriches our lives according to Napoleon Hill, one of the great thinkers of our time. He states in *Think & Grow Rich* that "being rich doesn't always have to do with money but…lasting and harmonious relationships."

Think and Be Happy

Every morning when you wake, begin by saying "thank you" for another day. Be grateful for all you can do. Appreciation often leads to satisfaction—one of the key ingredients in the recipe for happiness. Oprah Winfrey is credited with saying: "Be thankful for what you have; you'll end up having more. If you concentrate on what you don't have, you will never, ever have enough." Gratitude is a virtue that often leads to abundance.

Think and Be Happy

Consider this question posed by William Arthur Ward: "God gave us a gift of 86,400 seconds today. Have you used one to say thank you?"

Laugh. Find a laugh buddy and go for a giggle on a regular basis. Rent funny videos or DVDs. Listen to your favorite standup comic. Enroll in a laughter-therapy class which seems to be surfacing in many cities nowadays and some institutions including cancer treatment facilities such as the Seattle Cancer Treatment Center. There are numerous healing benefits of laughter. According to some studies, it can bolster the immune system, ease the tension in muscles and provide a feeling of well-being. There is power in laughter and it has been said that laughter is often the best medicine and certainly has allies in the medical world.

Keep your spirits under the influence of happiness by only allowing your mind to visit certain memory sites. When we log onto They-Really-Hurt-Me.com or They-Don't-Appreciate-Me.net, of course we're going to feel desolate and depressed and miss out on the beauty of life. If you find your mind diverting to those dreadful sites, immediately log back unto What-God-Has-Done-for-Me.com or ThoseWhoAppreciateMe.com or MyGodGivenDestiny.org or The-Things-and-People-who-Matter.com and remain in a state of serenity and peace.

Think and Be Happy

If you wish to experience happiness, think happy, positive, healthy thoughts all the time. It couldn't be more simple. There are some whose minds are tied up with distressing thoughts over situations they have little or no control over or they worry about the future that has not yet arrived and they wonder why they feel melancholy. Studies have shown that your feelings are often intertwined with your thoughts. The good news is we have the power to change the channel of thoughts in our minds at any given moment. As Abraham Lincoln once said, "People are as happy as they make up their minds to be."

Think and Be Happy

Enjoy the benefits of a smile. According to some research, a smile can *instantly* improve your mood in addition to providing many other health benefits. Smiling releases endorphins in the body: the "feel good" hormone. A smile is said to be the universal expression of happiness across all cultures. Try smiling this very moment. How does it make you feel?

Never forget that most great things have been accomplished through trial and error, or suffering and rejection. Every challenge provides an opportunity to do better, think better and become better.

Always remember that every day, and every moment you are alive, is a special occasion.

Think and Be Happy

Try distancing yourself from your moment of calamity. When overwhelming news strikes you head on, step away. Just for a moment, pretend you are a third-party observer. Clear your mind. Practice deep breathing. Focus on a positive outcome. See the situation from a different perspective—realizing that your troubles may not be as grandiose as you perceive. When you minimize your troubles, you maximize your control over the situation.

The first recipe for happiness is: "Avoid too lengthy meditations on the past," as French author Andre Maurois once scribed. Leave the past to rest in order to enjoy peace in the present.

Think and Be Happy

Your feelings are too precious and are often affected by whatever is playing on your mind's screen. Good news! As the director of your thoughts, you have the power to choose what will play, what you'll leave on the cutting room floor and what you will play on reruns. Let them be thoughts of empowerment, self-healing, positive self-image and health and happiness.

Think and Be Happy

Invite happiness into your life. Many of us do not allow enough room for joy because we are too tense being stressed out and unhappy. His Holiness, the Dalai Lama once said: "The basic thing is that everyone wants happiness, no one wants suffering. And happiness mainly comes from our own attitude, rather than from external factors. If your own mental attitude is correct, even if you remain in a hostile atmosphere, you feel happy."

Put God first in all that you do, think and feel. Studies have shown that those who are optimistic and religious and who practice "putting God first in their lives," tend to experience a calmer state of mind even in the midst of calamity. Hence the popular saying: "I'm too blessed to be stressed." When you feel yourself spiraling downward, try shifting your attention to God (or another higher power). Many Christian optimists do not worry themselves crazy when trouble strikes, they take on a hopeful outlook and press forward to good things. Many find comfort in the Bible verse Deuteronomy 31:8 (New King James Version) "...the Lord,...is the One who goes before you. He will be with you, He will not leave you nor forsake you; do not fear nor be dismayed."

As an unknown author once posed, "Don't tell God you have a big problem. Tell your problem you have a big God!"

Think and Be Happy

"As a man thinketh...so is he," proclaims Proverbs 23:7 in the Holy Bible as written by King Solomon, the wisest man ever to live. Your life becomes whatever you focus your thoughts on. Why contaminate your mind and your life by dwelling on negative, upsetting situations—ones that have long since expired? Don't waste precious time focusing on mediocrity. Experience joy. Let it shine through your actions. Whatever is in your thoughts, your mind, your heart and soul is what you truly become. Be mindful of what travels through your head. Ensure healthy, positive thoughts to assure you stay in the zone for happiness.

Think and Be Happy

We must value each blessed moment we have in our lifetime. We must not squander a second, a minute, an hour, a day. We need to tell those we love how we feel. And we must express that love by our actions towards them every single day.

When the colder side of reality bites, we have to dress ourselves warmly with a vest of hope, a sweater of faith, gloves of forgiveness and a double layer of optimism to shield us from the chill of trying times.

Many of the happiest people have one trait in common: a Spiritual First-Aid kit that may include a dose of hope, a blanket of support (they do not isolate themselves from loved ones), a shot of humor, and spiritual vitamins to take every morning as they greet each new day. Vitamin A for Acceptance of situations they cannot change. Vitamin B for Belief in themselves and their abilities to get through any calamity. Vitamin C for remaining Calm during chaos. Vitamin D for Determination. Vitamin E for Eliminating worries from their diet. Vitamin K for Kindness to others and to themselves. Additionally, research has shown that people who practice the virtues of happiness—optimism, forgiveness, gratitude, kindness, and joy—tend to live longer, healthier, and happier lives.

Think and Be Happy

There will always be boundless opportunities to make new friends, form closer bonds, achieve greater dreams, accomplish more, improve and do more in life. Never limit your thinking or your span of hope. The universe is a grand entity—there will always be more to explore as long as your mind is open and your heart is receptive to change.

You can implement positive changes in your life. Reflect on the highlights of your life and never forget the aspects that are going right (especially when things don't go as planned).

To keep the flow of happiness constant in your relationships sometimes it's more important to keep the peace than to be right.

Think and Be Happy

Another way to bring happiness into your thoughts is to be the recipient of happy news and uplifting stories. You can join a local happiness club by signing up on Websites such as The Happiness Club at *www.happinessclub.com,* the Secret Society of Happy People at *www.sohp.com,* the American Happiness Association at *www.americanhappiness.org,* or you can find happiness quotes from Inspirational Words of Wisdom at *www.Wow4u.com.* Think happy and be happy.

Think and Be Happy

Forgiveness opens the door for you to be forgiven as well. Most importantly, forgiveness liberates your heart, soul and mind to move forward and rise above toxic feelings of resentment. Forgiveness frees you to love and be loved. Rev. Dr. Martin Luther King, Jr. once said, "We must develop and maintain the capacity to forgive. He who is devoid of the power to forgive is devoid of the power to love." And Robert Mueller once posed, "To forgive is the highest, most beautiful form of love. In return, you will receive untold peace and happiness."

Think and Be Happy

Always look at the grand view of your life when dealing with difficulties. See the larger picture when tackling challenges with either situations or people. Recognize that each episode is a miniscule fraction of your entire journey and is not worth your peace of mind on your journey to happiness. Refuse to let anything sidetrack you on your excursion to greatness. As Deepak Chopra once proffered, "Nothing is more important than reconnecting with your bliss. Nothing is as rich. Nothing is more real."

Think and Be Happy

Keep in mind that YOU are the main player in your own life. You may have a plethora of secondary and supporting characters in your life—maybe even some minor characters—but don't trouble yourself too much in how others are playing their roles. What matters is how well you portray your character and how well you position your part.

Every night before you go to bed, practice emptying your mind of negative thoughts and perceptions of situations gone by. Replace with the high points of the day or the lessons learned that will add to your personal growth journey. Practice leads to perfection.

Think and Be Happy

The secret to happiness? A bad memory for bad experiences and a good memory for good experiences. Purge past thoughts that negate and refill with positive ones that elevate. As the late Honorable Robert (Bob) Nesta Marley once sang: "None but ourselves can free our minds."

Laugh at a joke, smile, think only healthy thoughts. Sink into a sentimental state of mind at least once a day.

Think and Be Happy

"We can do anything we want to do if we stick to it long enough," Helen Keller assured. Success could be eagerly waiting for you around the corner. Never give up hope. Walt Disney, the man, had a dream and he held on to it. After being fired from his job as a cartoonist, he went to set up his own business, even going bankrupt several times before succeeding. What if he had given up on his dream after his second bankruptcy? His critics are long gone but his name and his vision still live on!

Think and Be Happy

Forget insults, remember praises.

It's all a matter of perspective. View failure as nothing more than a steppingstone to success. Thomas Edison failed many times before he succeeded in inventing the lightbulb. But he never viewed himself as having floundered. When asked about it, Edison is credited with, "I have not failed 1,000 times. I have successfully discovered 1,000 ways to NOT make a light bulb."

"Happiness is not the absence of problems but the ability to deal with them," said H. Jackson Brown, author of *Life's Little Instruction Book*. In other words, we must remember that problems hold hidden value that makes us wiser and more refined the next time around as we extract the lesson from them. Remember that pressure creates diamonds.

In order to achieve true happiness, we need to take greater care of our mental health. This means staying mentally fit despite our circumstances. Pray, rest, meditate, relax, detox your mind of virulent thoughts, and experience inner-peace.

Roman philosopher Marcus Aurelius once wrote, "The happiness of your life depends on the quality of your thoughts." If we overload our minds with discouraging thoughts, it's unlikely we'll see the beauty of life. If we're not in optimal mental shape, it's difficult to enjoy the experiences in our lives.

Whenever trouble strikes, we must abandon feelings of hopelessness, eliminate negative thinking, exercise faith and keep our spirits soaring on the windmill of optimism.

Allow your spirit to shine brightly like the sun, regardless of the stormy weather you may encounter in your life.

Choose hope. Choose happiness. Flush out any doubts or negative notions by feeding yourself positive thoughts or spiritual words. There's a Chinese proverb that states: "As long as we have hope, we have direction, the energy to move, and the map to move by." In other words, hope is crucial to our survival. Theologian Emil Bruner once said, "What oxygen is to the lungs, hope is to the spirit." Hope keeps our spirit alive.

"A cheerful heart is good medicine, but a crushed spirit dries up the bones," states Proverbs 17:22. Doctors have often said that having a joyful spirit, positive mentality and optimistic outlook on life has played a key factor in the speedy recovery of some of their patients. Conversely, other studies have shown that some patients who have been pessimistic have slowed down their recoveries. We've all got that inner-warrior within us to rise above and overcome any trauma in our lives. It usually follows on the wings of a potent positive mentality and a joyful spirit that you can overcome any adversity. It's a matter of tapping into that resource.

"When you're at peace, you're in a position of power," preached popular televangelist Joel Osteen. When we have inner peace in the face of calamity, we have already won the battle.

Release all your fears and accept God's divine control in your life.

Shift your focus to the brighter side of everything and experience a complete state of euphoria and contentment. This practice makes for a good, instant mood-lifter. Do you see the glass half empty or half full? Every thing possesses at least a modicum of beauty. It's what you choose to search for in life that you will surely find.

Think and Be Happy

Think like a champion in the game of life. Play well. Believe in yourself—all the time, every time.

Think and Be Happy

Forgive those who have let you down and release the toxic thoughts about your hurtful feelings over the situation. Retain only beneficial thoughts and reflect on lessons learned.

Many of us waste time on petty worries or frivolities, but those who know the value of how limited time is seem to cherish every moment they have as a gift.

Think and Be Happy

We are the hero in our own life stories. We must act our unique parts and emerge with glory.

Think and Be Happy

Money does not buy happiness, but happiness can lead to money. A happy mind is a resourceful mind.

You can move on, grow wise, learn from all your silly mistakes, heal from all that has caused you pain, change profoundly, build resistance, take control, thicken your skin, mellow your soul, build confidence, find inner strength, earn back all your respect, succeed against the greatest odds, sew good seeds and reap from good deeds, taste sweet victory, get over things and get used to things, appreciate more and accomplish more with a powerful friend at your side. That friend? Time.

Express yourself clearly
Cleanse your thoughts daily
Rest well. Get enough sleep
Pray. Find inner peace
Network. Talk
Get out more. Walk
Enjoy your life, while you're here
Find the pleasures that make you care
Organize yourself
Take care of your health
Build new friendships
Salvage old relationships
See yourself in a better light
Be kind to others—all the time.
Rid yourself of pessimism
View all things with optimism.

Think and Be Happy

"We can rejoice too when we run into problems and trials for we know that they help us develop endurance. And endurance develops strength of character, and character strengthens our confident hope of salvation." ~Romans 5: 3-4 NLT Bible

"Being wronged is nothing unless you continue to remember it," wrote Confucius. In other words, the hurtful effects of insults can easily vanish from your mind when you simply stop thinking about them. Think of it this way, if you've been served a bad plate of ignorance from someone, don't take a double serving by holding on to that memory, too. Toss it out of your mind. Let it go and move on with your life into a state of joy.

There comes a time when we must peel away the layers of the past and embrace the newness, vibrancy and fresh new start of the upcoming day. Don't miss out on the gift of the present. Bask in it.

Every day we give birth to ideas about ourselves and the world in which we live. Labor your thoughts towards the favorable aspects of your life and watch happiness unfold before you.

When you wrap your child warmly every day with layers of your unconditional, healthy love before you send him out into the world, he will rarely feel the cold chill that often comes with life's changing seasons.

Remember three things: Thoughts are potent. They can manifest into reality. You will always be the Commander-in-Chief of your own thoughts.

Financial security. A satisfying dream career. Faithful friends. A loving spouse. Well behaved children. A beautiful home. Affordable vacations. Many times we postpone our feelings of happiness because we feel we need certain aspects or events in place first. As author H. Jackson Brown once wrote: "The true measure of success is not what you have, but what you can do without." Not convinced? Ancient Greek philosopher Aristotle, who happened to be a student of Plato and a teacher of Alexander the Great, once phrased it, "Happiness depends upon ourselves."

Happiness is not about whether people like or appreciate you. You'll never have one hundred percent approval from everyone. That's okay as long as you do your best and approve of yourself. Happiness is not about having stocks or bonds or a mansion or fabulous new set of wheels. It's about having a positive frame of mind whether you have these fleeting luxuries or not.

Think and Be Happy

Boost your spirits today by injecting at least one happy, memorable moment into your thoughts. Keep store of them and collect them like priceless jewels or precious coins to be admired and enjoyed.

Don't fret because you have lost a relationship, because you have been let down or because you have been disappointed. Consider instead, you have been given another round of wisdom to take you with you on your journey. As the Welsh proverb states: "Adversity and loss make a man wise."

Surround yourself with those who are good-minded. When you surround yourself with pessimistic people, their negativity can affect your own spirits. As a French proverb states: "Better to be seen alone than in bad company."

Think and Be Happy

The difference between happy people and unhappy people is never the situation. There are those in terrible conditions with high spirits and those who seem to have it all and still live in misery. It's about who has the ability to see the good in a situation and appreciate what they have. As Confucius once proffered: "Everything has beauty, but not everyone sees it."

"To the world you may be one person but to one person you may be the world" is a familiar quote by an anonymous author. For every person who may not appreciate you, there is someone who absolutely treasures your existence. It could be your spouse, loved one, child or parent, or close friend or someone whose life you touched in some special way. Be confident knowing that you are valuable and valued. Shift your focus to what really matters.

An ounce of understanding, a pinch of respect, and a dash of acceptance travel a long way when dealing with those close to you. Give what you wish to receive from others and enrich your relationships.

If you have any outstanding dreams, goals, desires, ask yourself what is stopping you from fulfilling them. When we accomplish greatness, a feeling of jubilance leaps into our hearts. As Proverbs 13:19 states: "A longing fulfilled is sweet to the soul."

It's okay to have down time. You can't be "up" every minute of every day. In fact, it has been well stated that you need the lows in life to appreciate the highs. Carl Jung, influential thinker, Swiss psychiatrist and founder of analytic psychology, once said: "Even a happy life cannot be without a measure of darkness, and the word happy would lose its meaning if it were not balanced by sadness. It is far better to take things as they come along with patience and equanimity." However, feeling down from time to time and staying down for an extended period of time are two different beasts. Always put your health first and seek advice from your family physician. Your inner peace and happiness are so worth the visit.

Think and Be Happy

Steer clear from those who try to drag your spirits into the ditch of unhappiness. Reverse from their driveway and drive off on your own road to inner peace. The place of despair is not an address you want to revisit any time soon.

Don't blame, ridicule, criticize, or stigmatize others. Stay away from negative talk. If you've been hurt, forgive and move forward. Don't stay in a mentally turbulent time warp. You draw time away from moving ahead in your life when you use it up to negate others. Additionally, you cannot experience genuine inner peace and happiness by focusing on negativity.

Think and Be Happy

Create a mini happiness action plan and stick to it. Typically, without a plan it's virtually impossible to reach a place by chance. For starters, think about what makes you happy or what will make you happy. Living below your means to create peace of mind? Vacationing once per year? Quiet time? Activities with your children? Being appreciative of the person you are? Appreciating your loved ones? Looking optimistically at situations instead of pessimistically? You decide. Each plan is as unique as each individual.

Think and Be Happy

Do not breathe life into a contaminated past by dwelling on it, thinking about it or revisiting it in your mind. Practice the fine art of letting go and releasing what is gone and done with.

Think and Be Happy

What makes some people habitually happy regardless of what they are facing while others appear chronically worrisome? Benjamin Franklin stated it well: "Happiness depends more on the inward disposition of mind than on outward circumstances."

Because every day is precious . . . Do whatever brings you joy and think the thoughts that bring you bliss. Every day will be paradise, an exciting adventure.

Be thankful. Truly thankful for all you have and can do. Give thanks for each blessed day we receive and for the ability to function normally, to breathe, and to make choices. I see so much in my line of work as a registered nurse that giving thanks in the morning to God for another day seems to come as natural as inhaling and invokes a good feeling. Be appreciative of each blessing. Take nothing for granted. Be content and experience abundance.

Spend a day at the beach. If not in the physical, then visualize or meditate on sitting comfortably under a colorful umbrella with your shades on and in a sun hat, on the sandy white beach sipping refreshing Strawberry Daiquiri punch. Hear the sensual sounds of the whooshing waves of the sea blue water gently splashing in the background. Feel the warmth of the sun rays pricking your skin, the delicate breeze whistling calmly through your locks of hair, the distant sounds of laughter of children playing on the shore. Visualize yourself reading a delicious book that whirls you away into another world, peeling your mind gently off your problems as they appear to melt away. What could be better than taking mini mental vacations on a regular basis? Yoga experts have often said that the art of positive visualizations have had healthy effects on the body such as lowering blood pressure among other things.

Think and Be Happy

Indulge yourself this very day with a collection of happy memories, happy movies, happy conversations. Keep it joyful and exuberant. Blend your day with a dose of uplifting music—watch your mood elevate. Music therapy has been used in healing for many years. In addition to "Don't Worry, Be Happy," another favorite "happy music" is "Happiness" by Billy Lawrence. The lyrics "Happiness...feels so good to be alive" says it all.

Give yourself a worry time limit much like a credit card. Don't overspend your time fretting about a given subject. For instance, designate twenty minutes a day, if you must, and whatever you do, don't exceed that limit. Try to slowly reduce your allowance every day. Whatever you do, don't go over your limit so you don't cut into your peace of mind time.

Release the cares and concerns of the day when you retire to bed each night. The day is done. Be still, unwind, indulge your mind with the gift of the moment. Take a deep breath and exhale your worries. Remember, when you have a good night you tend to have a good morning, too.

Allow a wave of positive emotions to wash over you as you dream and visualize pleasant experiences. This could include sitting on a beach reading a favorite book, playing golf, listening to your favorite tunes, or simply tuning out from the world and sinking into a luxurious scented bubble bath. Visualize goodness and experience good feelings.

Think and Be Happy

Dwell on achieving greatness in life and you will eventually achieve excellence with work and dedication. Let those positive thoughts resonate within your core and influence every thing you do. Napoleon Hill, author of the hugely popular classic, *Think & Grow Rich,* wrote that "success comes to those who become success conscious."

Happiness is a paradise we all desire to reach in our lives. Yet we keep ourselves from enjoying this experience when we load up with the onerous baggage of the past. Unload heavy burdens of worry and discontent and live joyfully in the moment. Get out of the danger zone and snap into the happy zone.

Think and Be Happy

Bobby McFerrin said it all in his cool, calming 80s hit song "Don't worry, be happy." The perfect piece of advice to follow on your journey to a life of happiness.

Think and Be Happy

We tend to put off feelings of pleasure and enjoyment in life by placing worries as our top priority, especially worries over which we have no control. Reverse the practice. Put off worrying for a change. Like Scarlett O'Hara in the movie Gone with the Wind, her famous line was "I'll think about that tomorrow" in response to how she was going to win back the man of her dreams. Put off worrying, live joyfully in the moment.

Think and Be Happy

Like an aircraft, our soul needs to fuel up to go the distance. Our spirits need to keep up and soar in the sky when faced with strife. We need to fuel up on inner strength, positive self-image, loving support and self-love. We need to keep our spirit ascending during the turbulent hours in our lives.

When you feel as if you are drowning in a sea of misadventures, remember the words of Helen Keller: "Character cannot be developed in ease and quiet. Only through experiences of trial and suffering can the soul be strengthened, vision cleared, ambition inspired and success achieved."

Whatever you go through, don't ever let yourself slip down. Grip on to whatever faith, courage, and hope you can. Whatever faces you head on. Cling to courage, peace, survival. With all your love and tenacity, inner strength and pertinacity. With all your warrior mentality, your grace and your vitality. Know your value—priceless, precious, timeless. Emerge from whatever mess you believe is treading you down. Emerge from your distress. Flourish. Blossom. Rebound.

Whatever makes you happy, makes you laugh, drives you, matters to you, motivates you, brings out the best in you, comforts you, elevates you, strengthens you or supports you, keep your mind on it, open your heart and your soul and embrace it, never lose sight of it, always nurture and dwell on it.

Think and Be Happy

Don't allow age, culture or beliefs to stop you from accomplishing your dreams. It's never too late. Consider black history heroine, Mary Shadd, who, during the 1800s, became Canada's first female reporter, editor, and publisher. Amidst the hardship of slavery, the trials of being black and a woman during that time period--a time when all the odds were stacked up against her, the widow and mother of two, became a school teacher, principal, lecturer, women's rights movement activist and the first female law student at Howard University in Washington, DC. She became a lawyer at sixty-years-old and continued her fight for a better world. A remarkable accomplishment, even by today's standards. And consider Estelle Rees Arroyo, who at ninety-two-years-old graduated from California State University, Sacramento, on May 22, 2009 with a bachelor's degree. Anything is possible once you hold on to a strong conviction to believe in yourself.

Sometimes not getting what you want, is a blessing in sleek disguise.

.

You are so much more than what troubles you, so much more than what lies around you. What lies within you is more beautiful, powerful, refined.

Life is a gift, be grateful for it.
The triumphs, the pains, the laughter, the aches.
Cherish every breath you take.
Be thankful for every day you wake.
Be thankful for each blessed hour.
Make time your friend. Respect her power.

True happiness comes from within, and there is power in positive thinking.

Think and Be Happy

If you had a choice between dwelling on negative thoughts that sink your spirits or a choice of focusing on thoughts that elevate you and propel you to achieve greatness and enjoy your life, on which would you choose to direct your energies? Most would say the latter. It is that simple. We always have choices. We can decide to dwell on being hopeless in situations or focus on having hope.

Think and Be Happy

When faced with mundane troubles, practice diverting your thoughts into the state of hopefulness, the zone of tranquility.

Be careful so as not to be consumed with negativity because it can overshadow your thinking and your life. In the morning, go through a spiritual detox regime. Meditate on a scripture or a positive message, mantra, or saying and continue to refuel your soul.

There's no better frame of mind than peace of mind during chaos.

Don't focus on the idea that you may be having a difficult day at work. Instead, shift your focus on how grateful you are to *have* a job in this day and age as well as how you are gifted with the ability to perform your job. Shifting your outlook on the advantages instead of the disadvantages improves your experiences.

Embrace hope. Hope is the driving force that keeps us moving forward in life. It propels us when we are faced with challenges. It is a crucial part of life and our feelings of well-being. Holding the belief that a positive outcome is possible despite our circumstances. Hope fuels perseverance and drives us to better ourselves. Never give up the belief that your situation can change.

Focus on solutions, not problems. View problems as challenges. Don't let your problems *define* you. Let your problems *refine* you. Don't focus on how you've been hurt. Instead, focus on how you can bounce back from the negative situation. Learn from your mistakes. Don't be burned by them. Nothing you have said or done is new under the sun. Everyone who breathes makes mistakes and mistakes typically make us wiser the next time around.

Elevate your confidence level. Coach yourself into believing in yourself.

When you feel as though your entire world has been capsized belly-up—practice flipping a negative into a positive to benefit from the value in the situation. For whatever you search, you will likely find.

We tend to focus on what we don't have; thus, we need to shift our focus towards what we do have. In fact, make a list of blessings and check it regularly.

Think and Be Happy

You are what you eat and you are what you think!

It is a blessing to be occupied with plenty of positive activities to do. A thoroughly occupied mind has little or no room to be consumed with petty annoyances.

Pursue your goals and dreams. Marianne Williamson, author of *A Course in Miracles,* states, "You'll find happiness when you're performing your life's function."

Keep this thought in mind by an unknown author: "Life is not about waiting for the storms to pass. It's about learning how to dance in the rain."

Think and Be Happy

What thoughts occupy your mind and time? Make sure they are valuable to your growth and happiness. Negative thoughts are too costly to your peace of mind. Hopeful thoughts add to your sense of well-being.

Don't allow anger to churn inside your mind. Release it. Replace it with pure, euphoric thoughts. Think health and happiness. Remember, as Ralph Waldo Emerson once stated: "For every minute you remain angry, you give up sixty seconds of peace of mind." While seemingly an insignificant amount of time, those seconds add up.

Think and Be Happy

"Our greatest glory is not in never falling but in rising every time we fall," Confucius once stated. Just because you messed up, slipped up, said the wrong thing or made the wrong move in the past, doesn't mean life ends there. Pick up, dust off and move on. The greatest achievers in history have gotten to where they were because they rose after earlier failures and mistakes. They prevailed. Rarely have they tried once and succeeded on the first try. You can achieve anything once you mentally commit to springing back on your feet.

"Nurture your mind with great thoughts, for you will never go any higher than you think."
-Benjamin Disraeli

If you can think about worries, you can think about happiness. If you can think about problems, you can think about solutions.

"You have not lived a perfect day...unless you have done something for someone who will never be able to repay you," said Ruth Smeltzer, as quoted in *What Jesus Meant*. The greatest blessing is when you give without expecting anything in return. Think of what a blessing you can give to another by a simple, kind deed.

Hidden in each difficulty lies a valuable lesson. Only the wise and open-hearted have the gift to find it.

Always keep this thought in mind: No negative situation or confrontation has to be a total loss once you can extract the gem of lesson from it to make yourself better the next time around. Living is about learning while growing and becoming.

Allow thoughts of happiness to consume your mind. Any adverse thoughts should be evicted immediately. Retain only thoughts that promote and nurture goodness and your sense of well-being.

If you want to receive something in life, you must pursue it. Make it your goal. Never cease trying.

When others try deliberately to annoy you, don't forfeit your peace in exchange for their disruptive behaviors. Hold on securely to your power, your inner-peace, your happiness. When you do this, healthy feelings surface and you are empowered once again.

Practice this ritual daily: Reflect only on healthy, positive thoughts to stimulate you into a happy mood. Dwell on good past experiences along with moments that bring a smile to your face. If your mind ever drifts towards unhealthy thoughts, quickly shift gears to the bright side of life to give yourself an instant mood lift.

Emerson once said: "For everything you have missed, you have gained something else." Believe that everything happens for a reason. Focus on lessons learned, growth experienced and faith renewed.

"Successful people keep moving forward. They make mistakes, but they don't quit," Conrad Hilton, founder of Hilton Hotels, once said. Keep on moving—don't be sidetracked or dissuaded from pursuing your dreams. Being human means making many mistakes. Those who succeed in life are those who learn from their mistakes and work to improve and press forward.

When someone annoys or upsets you, particularly without due cause, don't let him win twice by dwelling on what he's done to you. Instead, focus on how well you will handle it. Don't allow feelings of resentment to settle in your heart. Mentally flick off annoyances and shift your focus on how God can bring you through anything, can take care of anything under the sun and how you are protected by his angels.

The yellow brick road to happiness is paved with twists and turns, but it is easily travelled by those whose hearts are full of love, minds are full of forgiveness and whose spirits radiate appreciation for the little things in life.

We all desire happiness. This involves putting to rest feelings of fear and resentment and reviving feelings of hopefulness and optimism.

Think and Be Happy

Become a person of value and you may always experience success and abundance.

Think and Be Happy

Try this exercise: Think only beautiful, hopeful, empowering thoughts for one minute, then try this for one hour and then one day. Make this a habit. Any negative thoughts that may creep into your mind, mentally purge them and replace with healthy thoughts. You'll soon experience happiness beyond your wildest imagination.

Being happy is the sweetest victory. During the most troubling times, keep shining, keep smiling, remain in a state of inner-peace and joy.

Happiness usually keeps company with friends called Hope, Inner-Peace and Forgiveness.

You always have control over what you experience within, your thoughts, your feelings, and your emotions . . . regardless of your circumstances.

I *can* do it!—Try these magical words and apply them to your dreams, your desires, your hopes. Possibilities can quickly transform into realities.

Think and Be Happy

Sometimes we need to pilot our thoughts through turbulence by maneuvering our actions towards being still and allowing the flow of peace to be experienced within.

Many of us heat to a boiling point when others do us wrong. It happens. Practice monitoring your temperature gage. Practice keeping cool on the hot seat. Keep your spirit together. Inner-peace during chaos is the most valuable gift we can take with us on our lifelong journey.

Treasure your relationships and recognize they are a precious gift from God. May you always have a constant and abundant flow of God's blessings.

Make it your aim to always do your best, feel your best, give your best every time. You will more than likely reap the benefits when you sow seeds of goodness and greatness everywhere you go.

Your life is whatever you choose to concentrate on. Happiness is merely a thought away. Always remember that. Most people who lead happier lives keep a treasury of good thoughts in their mind.

True success and triumph are not about having more, but about becoming more.

Think and Be Happy

Don't forget to take good care of your mind's hardware. Nourish your brain with a well-balanced diet including fresh fruits and vegetables. For example, studies show that an apple a day really does keep the doctor away by boosting your immune system, providing energy, aiding in digestion and helping to reduce the chance to acquire many illnesses through the release of antioxidants. In addition to good nutrition, adequate rest and exercise are crucial for your brain.

We are like spiritual magnets in our experience in life. Whatever we focus on, dwell on or embrace tends to gravitate towards us. Proverbs 4:23 tells us, **"A**bove all else, guard your heart, for it affects everything you do." Guard your heart and soul from negativity and destructive emotions. Focus on good, healthy, positive experiences and favorable things and draw to you what you do want in life, not what you don't desire.

Focus your time, your energy and your thoughts on those who appreciate you, not those who do not appreciate the person you are. Studies have shown that for every person who dislikes you, no matter what you do to win their approval, there is someone who adores you just because you are you. One of the greatest time wasters is dwelling on the negative people, so try focusing on the positive relationships you have and enjoy and make the best out of your precious time on earth.

Keep on moving on in life. Like the hands of time, don't stop. If you scan the pools of successful achievers in the world, you will see a common denominator. They may have been knocked down, failed or derailed in life, but they keep on making hits, keep on singing, acting, building, making deals, teaching, laughing, sharing their natural gifts with the world. That is their secret to keeping afloat and moving forward with the current. Learn from the best and keep moving ahead.

Think and Be Happy

Be grateful for all that you can do. From the simple to the divine. The ability to breathe, think, walk, read and millions of other tasks. When we think about all the good aspects that help us run smoothly in life and we have and express our gratitude to God, we realize how richly blessed we truly are. As Brother David Steindl-Rast once said: "Gratefulness is the key to a happy life that we hold in our hands, because if we are not grateful, then no matter how much we have we will not be happy -- because we will always want to have something else or something more."

Allow this thought to settle in your mind: More than likely, you have already won the lottery. Maybe not the state lottery but the genetic lottery. Think about the fact that you can read this book, breathe, think freely. Many are without basic skills that we take for granted every day. Maybe it's your wonderful family you were born into, the life of freedom you were born into, your gifts, talents, abilities, siblings and many more. Be grateful for your non-monetary winnings and cherish what you have been blessed with by chance.

When faced with difficulties, never let your guard down. Tap into your inner resources and gain your strength and sense of well-being.

Practice the art of shedding the weight of pressure. Don't accumulate it with each negative situation. Shake it off. Press forward to better experiences.

Don't forget to replenish your soul with good sentiments about yourself and those who care about you. Too many times we get depleted as we spend ourselves emotionally through the day. Refill through being still, meditations, positive imagery, deep breathing, exhaling worries, prayer, self-love, reactivating faith and unconditional self-acceptance.

Keep a treasure trove of blissful memories and empowering thoughts at your disposal. Whenever negative emotions try to surface, replace the negative thoughts that bring it on with positive, healthy, hopeful ideas.

You need to take on the role of spiritual mechanic in your own life. If you've got a leak in your self-esteem, tune up with assertive, empowering concepts that begin with "I can…" or "I will…" Use the right tools at the right time, such as a phone to talk to a good friend, a book to read to take your mind off your worries, the art of networking, socializing, resting, meditating, exercising, relaxing, eating well. Many of us wonder why we don't have the energy to press forward during difficulty. It's important to remember that life has to be maintained like a garden and tuned up like an automobile to give us the beauty and best mileage.

One of my favorite Dr. Seuss quotes said it best: "Be who you are and say what you feel because those who mind don't matter and those who matter don't mind."

Think and Be Happy

"To wake up in the morning is a gift from God," wrote J.E. King. We must not forget the first blessing of the day. Life. The ability to wake and greet the new day. A new beginning. Psalm 118: 24 states: "This is the day the Lord has made; let us rejoice and be glad in it."

When we have a flow of good energy in our hearts and we aim to make others happy—we cannot keep happiness from our own selves. Mark Twain once said: "The best way to cheer yourself up is to try to cheer somebody else up." Who can you cheer up this very day?

Think and Be Happy

Life is a gift and the present is the time to cherish it.

Embrace your God-given talents. We all have unique skills and abilities. In fact, it has been said that people are equipped with at least 500 to 800 skills and abilities! We are all capable of doing many things. It could be that you are an exceptional speaker, listener, writer, vocalist, or maybe your congenial nature or charm in addition to technical skills are your crowning glories. Focus on what you excel at and share those gifts with others.

Dr. Seuss once said: "Don't cry because it's over, smile because it happened." When you look at the grand scheme of existence, you realize that every experience in life is temporary. All things must come to pass eventually. When you look at the experiences as a gifted blessing on your journey in life and take with you the lessons and good memories that make you smile, that have shaped you into who you are, you realize that moving forward is okay.

Be careful what subject holds your undivided attention or drifts into your mind. Let it be empowering thoughts to uplift you.

Allow the miracles of each day like breathing, thinking, or being one with nature to captivate you and inspire you.

The quickest way to rid your mind of toxic thoughts, thereby ridding your body of toxic emotions, is to practice mentally flushing out the negative perceptions of situations and replenish immediately with a healthy dose of faith, gleeful perceptions and acceptance. For example, if someone cuts you off in traffic, you have two choices: (A) You can believe he or she did it intentionally and decrease your peace of mind time by harboring feelings of resentment or (B) You can believe he or she must have had some sort of an emergency and didn't mean to cut you off. The latter explanation induces a feeling of well-being within you.

There's no better boost for the self-esteem than having accomplishments.

Join a club or forum with people who share similar interests. Network. Being around like-minded individuals, doing what you love is blissful for the mind and soul.

Remember that you are the most important person in your life. Take supreme care of yourself. If you don't, who do you think will?

Think and Be Happy

Why not designate a make-time-for-myself day or moment and meditate or do whatever it is that relaxes and fulfills you.

Give yourself a Happiness Makeover complete with an attitude lift, problem peel and ego massage.

Think and Be Happy

Live for the respect of a single person in your life. You!

Think and Be Happy

What people think about you should not be your prime concern. What matters most is how *you* feel about yourself. You're the one who is living in your skin and will be until the final chapter in your life's story.

We often tend to develop a form of selective amnesia of good events when heated arguments surface with loved ones. Always remember the good traits of your significant other and why you chose his or her company. Never allow a cloudy moment to overshadow an entire relationship.

Secure your happiness with first-class beliefs about yourself and the person you've become. Keep a stock of good thoughts and refill during difficult moments.

When your child tells you "I love you" or a loved one expresses his or her affection towards you, cling to those moments like Velcro. Let it influence you and remind you of what truly matters.

Be mindful where you spend your mental energies. Let whatever you focus on in life advance you to happiness and inner-peace on your spiritual growth journey.

Think and Be Happy

Don't worry if things are not going as planned for you despite your best efforts. Everything happens when it is due to happen, not sooner, not later. We must be confident in this and having faith is necessary on our mission to happiness. Don't worry about others—everyone's journey is unique to him or her. Continue to work towards your goal knowing that you will rise again in due time. Ecclesiastes 3:1-8 in the Bible says it all:

> To everything there is a season,
> a time for every purpose under the sun.
> A time to be born and a time to die;
> a time to plant and a time to pluck up that which is planted;
> a time to kill and a time to heal ...
> a time to weep and a time to laugh;
> a time to mourn and a time to dance ...
> a time to embrace and a time to refrain from embracing;
> a time to lose and a time to seek;
> a time to rend and a time to sew;
> a time to keep silent and a time to speak;
> a time to love and a time to hate;
> a time for war and a time for peace.

Everything in life takes practice, including survival skills. Practice keeping yourself together in the midst of difficulty until it becomes natural—even second nature. Self-heal from insults, guard your aspirations from being dented by personality collisions you may encounter. Embrace hope and happiness until it flows through you in every and all circumstances.

We don't need to be dependent on another human being to fulfill our soul purpose and destiny in life. As famous televangelist Joel Osteen once preached: God has equipped each and every one of us with the right blend of ingredients to be all that we should be in life.

Focus your mental energies on the desires of your heart. The stuff that builds you up, not the decay that breaks you down. Be mindful of the type of thoughts playing in your mind at any given moment.

Cling to the people and experiences in life that are good to you and for you in life, those that bring you baskets of happiness and unfiltered joy.

Think and Be Happy

When you feel as if you are detouring into a path of negativity, shift your attention to God, the beauty of life, moving forward, being all that you can be in life. Bask in the splendid miracle of living. Let it sustain you through hard times.

176

Bank your time and mental energies wisely. Spend your efforts and thoughts on what will uplift you, propel you forward in life, build you up, mold you strong. When we bank our time and thoughts prudently in positive experiences, we tend to reap a surplus of happiness.

Engage your mind with healthy perceptions. It has untold powers that can shape the life you live.

You can build your mind power everyday. Read, solve puzzles, keep your brain active by increasing knowledge and enhancing memory abilities.

Activate the happy-feel-good drug released into your system from the brain naturally by exercise, play, laughter, engaging in fun activities, excitement. Endorphins are nature's hormone that promote health, happiness and a sense of well-being. It has been said that this innate chemical in our bodies also acts as a natural pain reliever that creates feelings of euphoria. The question remains, why aren't we tapping into this natural resource more often?

Splurge on yourself when it comes to showering yourself with self-respect, self-improvement, internal happiness. Keep spending energy on becoming a better and a happier you. You are worth it!

If you're distressed about a situation, slip into a more comfortable frame of mind by diverting your thoughts to solutions, realizing that every situation has a way out. Anything is possible once we believe and never relinquish hope.

Think and Be Happy

It's quite normal to feel down from time to time. The important thing is to never stay down. Sometimes we need the low experiences to appreciate the high points.

Recognize a bad experience as a temporary one. A bad day does not signify a bad life.

Collect memories of inspiring moments and store them in
your mind. Draw from your resources to elevate your spirit
when the situation seems discouraging.

The special materials you need to build a fulfilling, rewarding life are located in one special place—within you. In your heart, your mind, your soul. As Dr. Norman Vincent Peale once encouraged: "Believe that all the resources you need are in your mind. That's a formula that actually works!"

Believe in yourself and your abilities to achieve your dreams and mere possibilities can quickly transform into potent realities.

Think and Be Happy

You may not always filter the information that enters your mind, but you can choose what information remains. Dwell on thoughts beneficial to your personal growth journey and sense of well-being.

Many of the happiest people in the world have one characteristic in common—a determination to choose happiness over self-pity regardless of their situations.

Release all your fears and accept God's divine presence in your life.

You have the right to be happy today and every day thereafter and to enjoy a sense of well-being regardless of your condition. Always stand up for and assert your right.

.

Faith and Hope—with these two virtues by your side, you will feel empowered to live your life in confidence.

There will always be opportunities to turn your life around and become the best that you can be. Be confident in your abilities and a forgiving friend called TIME.

Problems are valuable blessings in disguise. They allow us to develop character and provide us an opportunity to improve ourselves while appreciating when things are going well for us.

Allow good thoughts to flow through your mind and your soul will be forever in harmony with life.

Unleash your inner champion—we are all built with the potential for greatness.

When navigating yourself through life's challenges, equip yourself with a dose of inner courage, a peace-driven mind, and thoughts focused on valuing the journey as a learning experience.

Savor this gift called the moment. Live in it completely and purposefully. Life consists of nothing more than moments and memories. Create many, many happy ones.

Think and Be Happy

When you are able to wake up in the morning, breathe, think, make choices—consider yourself richly blessed. Take nothing for granted.

It has been said that the mind is not the master of the body but the servant to the body—doing exactly what you tell it to do. Channel empowering commands.

Sometimes we need an emotional shield of hope when faced with gusts of negative energy and a torrential downpour of problems. Hope is a virtue that is always at our disposal.

Feast on happiness. Those who acquire a taste for experiencing happiness tend to satisfy their cravings and drink in success every time.

Think and Be Happy

Don't allow any circumstance or person to put a dent in your enthusiasm for life.

Think and Be Happy

Always aim to clear up any outstanding misunderstandings in your relationships.

To feel good, do good. To live good, be good.

Having peace of mind and a happy, hopeful spirit is a luxury we can all afford.

Plant seeds of hope in our children so that they may experience a sense of well-being on their personal growth journeys.

Wash away negative experiences of the day from your mind. Be confident in knowing that a new day brings new experiences and a new beginning.

An unsinkable, hopeful spirit can sustain you for a long distance as you sojourn on your personal growth journey through life.

True success should not be measured by what you have but by what you become within.

Think and Be Happy

Set your mentality to be a champion driver in life, not an idler in the back seat.

Little annoyances that may cross our paths during the day can simply melt away like the falling snow when we keep our spirit warm with optimism.

Think and Be Happy

When we open our hearts and souls to forgiveness, faith and gratitude, we may watch the blessings flow and wonderful experiences pile up in our lives.

Think and Be Happy

Too many people remain uptight over their problems—like a chameleon that changes its skin color to match its environment. We must practice the art of resilience— bouncing back. Resist sinking into the depths of our circumstances. Practice lifting our spirits higher than what troubles us.

Fall in love with life every day over and over again and experience life loving you in return.

Think and Be Happy

Simply STOP thinking of a counterproductive thought. Concentrate on something that produces happiness or promotes your sense of well-being. When a negative thought creeps into your mind, redirect it with a positive word such as God, Love, Peace, Happiness. It has been said that the average human can think of many thoughts but only one at a given time—even if it is for a second. Keep healthy thoughts at the forefront of your mind at any given moment.

There is a saying: Children spell love T-I-M-E. Treasure the time you spend with your child. Time has a greater value than material gifts—a genuine asset that cannot be recycled, exchanged or returned.

According to the law of attraction, whatever we choose to dwell on we draw into our lives like a magnetic attraction. Make sure you fix your focus on what you really want in life, what will be beneficial to you—not on what you don't want.

Ecclesiastes 7:14 is one of many powerful verses in the Bible that is self-explanatory. Find comfort in the words knowing that everything happens for a reason. "When things are going well, enjoy yourself, and when they are going poorly, consider this: God has designed the one no less than the other so that we should take nothing for granted."

We tend to disrupt our peace when we dwell on those who have hurt or wronged us. Well, today and every day from this moment forward only focus your precious time and energy on those worthy of our attention, those who genuinely care about us, uplift us and appreciate who we are. Be richly blessed.

Sometimes we have to simply let things slide off our backs—including insults—allow them to slip off your back and melt on the ground.

Think and Be Happy

Don't allow the light of your inner-peace to be dimmed by a negative comment or occurrence. This is the time for it to shine bolder and brighter.

When you choose to partner with faith, hope and love—these three virtues, you are in a position of power and peace.

In the duration of your life, fuelling up on hope, endurance and confidence makes the journey that much easier and your mindset that much stronger.

When you choose to spoon out forgiveness, understanding and compassion towards others, you can't help but notice a lighter load that surrounds your heart and soul. Another ingredient in the recipe for a happier life—we tend to receive back what we feed to others.

Never forget that you possess the power to dilute any heated situation by infusing a little peace, a little understanding and a little respect.

Practice eradicating thoughts from your mind that distress you. Then replenish with thoughts that promote feelings of happiness. Much like art, any skill can be mastered through dedication and practice. As the saying goes: Where there's a will, there's a way.

Another ingredient in the recipe for happiness—halt the habit of conjuring up old, distressing memories. When the day is done—be done with it. Deliberately refuse to give any more air time in your mind to thoughts of regret. Life is too precious to waste on pettiness.

Be selective about what you play in your mind because it affects your entire outlook on life and your body. Think up— not down.

Keep your mind clear from muddy memories. Focus on thoughts of love, hope, happiness, growth, respect. These hold valuable properties to sustain your spirit through difficult times.

Time is the most precious valuable commodity we have. Once it is deducted from our daily balance of hours, it can never be retrieved. So spend each minute wisely and ensure those we love have a generous dollop of our time.

As we go through a series of dramas in our lives—we become more skilled at playing our roles, picking up on cues, acting appropriately, solving problems, improvising when and where necessary. Obstacles are truly a blessing in sleek disguise.

When we practice the art of radiating kindness and well-wishes to others, those friendly rays miraculously travel back to the source—You!

Like a bank of hope, you can only withdraw from your mind what you put into it. Think of what you are depositing to your mind's memory bank. Deposit good, healthy, productive thoughts and withdraw pleasant feelings and optimism to get you through each day.

We are shaped by our experiences, negative and positive. Decide how you will allow each situation to mold you.

Just as we nourish our bodies every day, we must also feed our minds with hopeful, healthy, and empowering thoughts on a daily basis. With this, you will never starve for affection or go hungry for acceptance.

When you nourish your mind with good thoughts, you tend to radiate good vibes.

Don't allow troubles to chip away at your spirit. Instead, allow them to build up your spiritual immune system by extracting the value from the lessons they bring to you.

Carve out time for yourself to discover your hidden talents, get in touch with your inner self and enjoy the simple pleasures in life that bring you bliss.

Believe in the power of possibilities. Believe that you can accomplish anything to which you set your mind.

Money isn't everything. Love, happiness, good health, inner-peace, relaxation, support from loved ones, positive self-esteem, satisfaction with what you have, and having hope are a few treasures that enhance and add value to our lives.

Think and Be Happy

Beginning today, make it a habit to count your blessings everyday. You may not have all that you want but absolutely nothing is stopping you from making the best of what you do have. Focus on what's going right in your life. You'll begin to experience feelings of appreciation, happiness and unfiltered joy. As legendary coach, John Wooden, once said: "Things work out best for those who make the best of how things work out."

Regardless of your situation, try visualizing a positive outcome for whatever adversity you are going through. According to the Law of Attraction, we tend to attract what we focus our energies on.

It's not about what happens to you but what happens within you that matters most in your personal growth journey through life. Good news: What happens within you is something you always have control over.

Knowledge is power and we must strive to accomplish more every day regardless of our situations.

Allow your spirit to shine brightly like the sunlight regardless of the stormy weather you may encounter along your personal growth journey. As visionary Anthony J. D'Angelo stated: "Wherever you go, no matter what the weather, always bring your own sunshine." And as William Arthur Ward once said, "A cloudy day is no match for a sunny disposition. "

The greatest photo album happens to be stored in your hippocampus. It has been said that we have the capacity to store three trillion facts in our brains. Collect happy memories by creating memorable moments with loved ones to draw upon later for inspiration.

Before you believe in anything or anyone, believe in yourself.

We've all got that inner warrior within us, to rise above and overcome any obstacle or battle. It's a matter of tapping into our inner resource.

You need to know where you want to go in life before you get there.

Think and Be Happy

Affirm what you wish to experience in life. Daily affirmations are a glorious way to boost your spirits. A few listed below can help you through your day:

I will cherish every precious moment as a gift from God.
I am healthy in every way.
I am very happy.
My heart is filled with gratitude for everything in my life.
I have an avalanche of bountiful blessings flowing my way from every direction.
I am always in a state of joy.
I am optimistic about my future.
I have an unlimited supply and rich source of hope within.
My happiness depends on within, not on external events.
I embrace all good things in my life.
I am thankful for every blessing in my life.
I forgive those who've let me down, and I release toxic thoughts about them—I will reflect on each experience as a lesson.
I am filled with inner grace, tranquility, optimism, goodness.

Continue…

Think and Be Happy

Continued...

I will always have abundance of good things.

have the power to move forward and improve after setbacks.

I am a champion in the game of my life.

I have the power to choose my moods regardless of my circumstances, and I choose to be happy today.

I will always shift my focus to the brighter side.

I will file and store good, healthy thoughts in my memory bank.

I will treasure my relationships and realize they are blessings from God.

I am protected by God's angels.

I release all my fears and accept God's divine ruling in my life.

I am confident that God supplies all my needs.

I embrace faith, healing, forgiveness, happiness.

Mistakes are another unlikely blessing. They help us to grow through the pain of error. To become wiser the next time around. But more than anything, mistakes happen. We are human. According to the book *Angel Courage*, the author encourages, "May you always make mistakes, just not the same ones." And as the Pope (John Paul) once said, "People should never be ashamed to say they have been wrong, which is saying, in other words, they are wiser today than yesterday."

Hard work + dedication + perseverance – self-doubt = achievement.

Henry Ford once offered, "Obstacles are those frightful things you see when you take your eyes off your goal." Never peel your eyes off your destiny, your dreams, your desires, your goals. Keep pressing forward and recognize little annoyances as distractions to be dismissed while you press forward to greatness.

We must treasure the simplicities in life such as the breath we are able to draw, the touch of our child's hand, the warmth of affection from those close to us. It has been said that we need to "Enjoy the little things in life, for one day you may look back and realize they were the big things."

Sometimes it is difficult to see the light in a dark situation, but that is when it is absolutely necessary.

Think and Be Happy

When trouble strikes, don't be discouraged, be determined to get through in one piece and learn from the experience as you travel on your personal growth journey. May problems make you wiser, stronger and appreciative of the good things in your life.

Follow clergyman and author Charles R. Swindoll's 90/10 principle wherever you go in life. In fact, allow this principle to travel with you in every situation. "Life is 10 percent what happens to you and 90 percent how you react to it."

Don't let your age be a deterrent from enjoying every aspect of your life. You're as old (or young!) as you feel. Look for ways you can work towards a life filled with hope and happiness.

As someone once explained: "It matters not how long we live, but how we live." How are you choosing to live your life today? In regret over the past, in anticipation of the future or in enjoyment of the present moment?

Think and Be Happy

There'll be people who let you down,
Don't appreciate you,
talk behind your back,
Torment you, test you
and ultimately lose your trust.

And for every one,

There'll be people,
who sincerely appreciate you,
Encourage you, believe in you,
Care about you, are there for you,

Praise you behind your back,
Love you unconditionally,
And always lift you up.
When you're up against those who are unkind
Remember the angels in your life
Who have been by your side.

Never forget that love means "in spite of" because no one is perfect. Love means truly loving a person in spite of his faults. Love is a powerful emotion that unites all the positive human emotions. It's the most valuable gift you can give another human being, yet it costs very little, if anything.

Successful achievers don't necessarily follow a path, they make one. In 1981 when six-year-old Kevin Weekes began playing hockey in Toronto, the National Hockey League still didn't have its first black goalie. That did not dissuade him from pursuing his dream. In 1993 he was "ranked the second goalie in the world for the NHL draft." Today, Weekes plays for the New Jersey Devils with an impressive record behind him. Create your own path. If you want to reach a destination but you don't see any clear marked way of getting there or footsteps to follow, then start making foot prints in the sands of life.

Forgiveness is a freedom we can't afford not to have. The Holy Bible says: "Blessed are the merciful, for they shall obtain mercy."

Think and Be Happy

We keep those, who've passed on, alive
By remembering all the good times

Honoring their past lives
And how they've touched our lives

We know they must move on
Their work here has been done

Back into the hands of God
Where they can now watch over us

Memories keep loved ones alive
It's memories of them that will never die.

Think and Be Happy

Create as many happy moments with your loved ones because one day—they'll become happy memories we can cherish forever.

Let your life sing of joy and hope—even amidst adversities—a soul that is able to blossom amidst a dark moment—is the most beautiful, brightest creature.

If you have a dream, work hard and plan your way. Any place worth going is worth a carefully thought out plan. Gather resources, network and reach out to others. Any dream is possible. But most of all, never give up and never stop learning.

You need to know where you want to go in life before you get there. Having an idea of what you want and a solid plan on how to get there is not only beneficial but absolutely necessary.

Dare to succeed against the odds. Dare to rise above your adversity. Never lose hope—no matter how long it takes! Believe in yourself even when you feel alone in your battles.

Nothing trumps a winning attitude. It's not about what happens to us but our reaction to it that matters. Doctors have often said that attitude played an important part in the recovery of some of their patients.

No matter what you're going through, know that God can carry you through. As an unknown author famously stated, "If God brings you to it, He will bring you through it." Have confidence in this belief and watch as hope transforms you. When you believe with your heart and soul, anything is possible.

Think and Be Happy

I've always said that life becomes simple when you follow
simple rules, and this is what I think:

If you fall down, get back up.
If you get hurt, aim to recover.
If you start to feel down, bounce back up.
If you mess up, clean up.
If you want love, give love.
If you want a friend, be a friend.
If you feel alone, pick up the phone.

If you've been disgraced, move on with grace.
If you've been betrayed, forgive and forget.
If you fail today, succeed tomorrow.
If you've gambled and lost, learn and move on.
If you ever feel lost, turn to God.

We all have aspects of our lives that can serve as inspiration to others. Give the best of yourself where possible and enrich the lives of others as you enrich your own.

Think and Be Happy

As Ralph Waldo Emerson once said, "Our strength grows out of our weaknesses." We all have deficits. One woman who was ridiculed as a child decided to use her own disability as a steppingstone to help others like herself while educating those that it's not what you can't do that matters but what you can still do. She became a successful movie talent agent. Once again, it's all a matter of attitude as an indicator of how your life will turn out, not so much your situation.

Think and Be Happy

Your phone hasn't rung today, but have you rung someone else's phone? Be the friend, the daughter, the sibling, the parent, or the soul-mate you desire in others. Give the love you want to receive from others. If you want love, give love. If you want joy, give joy. Give it often, expecting nothing in return. By expressing genuine kindness to others, we enrich our own lives.

Be the Friend You Desire to Have. Friendship is God's most precious gift. Be the friend you've always wanted to have to someone else without expecting anything in return. As Gloria Steinem once said, "Far too many people are looking *for* the right person, instead of trying to *be* the right person." Maintaining good friendships is another key ingredient in the recipe for deep, lasting happiness.

Have a positive force or motivation driving your life (whether good people or religion) or you may be driven around to places you may not want to go. And before you believe in anything, or anyone, believe in yourself. According to a University of Toronto study that reveals a distinct difference in the brain of believers and non-believers of God, believing in God (or a higher power) can help block anxiety and minimize stress.

Engage in joyful planning. In other words, set fun goals for yourself. Whether it is buying a newer car, finding your dream home, adding a new gadget to your collection, finding inner-peace, or taking a much needed vacation. This way, you'll rarely dwell on the obstacles and you're more likely to endure the bad times knowing that something good is coming. Even if it's just looking forward to your days off to relax and unwind or catching a movie at the cinema. Look forward to something. Anything.

Forgive those who have done wrong to you. When you forgive—you release toxic thoughts and hurtful emotions as you move forward. Forgive yourself as well. None of us are perfect, but we can learn valuable lessons from our mistakes.

Make time for the people close to you. They say that if you're too busy for family or friends, then you are just too busy. Why not designate Friday or Saturday evening as Family Fun Night? Rent a DVD or go to the theatre. Order take-out. Dine at a fine restaurant. Get into the habit of giving joy to others. As the saying goes, "Happiness is contagious, be a carrier."

Develop Your Own Signature Phrase by which to live. I've noticed the habits of many optimists who have developed their own signature phrases as their personal anthems. They often reply to negative circumstances by saying: "No worries," "I'm cool," "I'm too blessed to be stressed," "It'll pass," or "I'll get over it," as an antidote to mentally corrosive situations—a boost for their spirits. They shrug off any negative situations and are able to move on with their lives. They bounce back quickly when they get knocked down. Develop your own signature phrase or borrow from the above-mentioned examples. The more you tell yourself something—the more you believe it and the more you act on it subconsciously.

Think and Be Happy

A person's life is what his or her thoughts make of it. Your life is whatever you choose to focus on. As Dr. Norman Vincent Peale once said: "Change your thoughts and you change your life." You have the power to choose your moods and control your feelings. Your mind controls your world as you see it. Keep your thoughts favorable especially about yourself. Negative thoughts pull you down and can affect your well-being. Positive thoughts can uplift anyone out of a dark moment. I remember a story I read about 1930s child star, Shirley Temple, who was told by directors to think of something terrible like never seeing her mother again to draw real tears for a scene. This was a technique that actually worked with her. You can see what the power of concentrating on a particular issue can do to our emotions and how it can affect our bodies. If we are feeling down, it is most likely because we are thinking of something that is depressing to us. If negative thoughts enter your mind, switch the "thought" channel and think of something more positive. Or flash the word God or Peace or Love across the window of your mind.

There's no better frame of mind than peace of mind during chaos.

Think and Be Happy

Laugh. Laughter has been dubbed the best medicine, time and time again. Have a sense of humor. But remember the saying that it's not just the ability to tell a joke but the ability to take one. Not only is giggling a good muscle relaxant, it also releases endorphins, the body's own "happy drug," into your blood stream. Before anyone else can laugh at you, learn to laugh at yourself when you make a simple mistake. If you are ever at a loss for a good reason to laugh try *www.Google.com* and search for Websites on good clean jokes such as *www.ahajokes.com*. This is one of many Websites that provide thousands of clean jokes, funny pictures and humorous cartoons.

Practice the fine art of painting a brilliant portrait of yourself and your world. Enjoy the blissful masterpiece you've created on your happiness easel.

Think and Be Happy

Meditate on this quote: "There are no hopeless situations, only people who think hopelessly." Every situation has the potential for learning, growth and wisdom. Make the most out of every occurrence and no time will be wasted.

Sweep out negative thoughts from your mind and clean up old thoughts of self-doubt. What you'll have left is a clear, serene state of inner-peace.

Your life becomes influenced by whatever you choose to focus on. You have the power to focus on whatever you choose.

You hold the power to make up your mind, any way you choose. Get into the mindset to enjoy every day regardless of the characters you pass by or regardless of the scenes of life that are playing right now. You'll be surprised at how much you enjoy your own life when you don't give power to outside situations to create feelings of well-being within you. Be like the sun, shine within—regardless of life's weather conditions.

The best present is within you. The greatest present is to unwrap the gift of true divine love, opening the fountain of ever-flowing happiness from your soul to everyone. Your very being, body, mind and soul encompass a gift that is irreplaceable and invaluable to the receiver.

Have a nice day, unless you have other plans, one author famously stated. When we make a decision to be content with a situation or a person, miracles transpire. We tend to see what we wish to find. A story about a senior citizen who was told she had a place available became excited and said she loved it even though she hadn't viewed it. She had already made up her mind. And her experiences at her new home became filled with promise; she always saw the good aspects. Conversely, when you seek out and expect only negatively, you blind yourself to seeing the good side. There is always good and bad in every situation. Always keep your vision clear and your expectations optimistic if you want to experience joy and happiness.

Meditate on this statement by Ralph Waldo Emerson: "Finish each day and be done with it. You have done what you could; some blunders and absurdities have crept in; forget them as soon as you can. Tomorrow is a new day; you shall begin it serenely and with too high a spirit to be encumbered with your old nonsense."

Mother Teresa once preached, "Peace starts with a smile." Always wear a smile as part of your attire and experience joy as you share enjoyment with others.

"If God closes one door, he opens another," as the famous adage states. The trouble is, we gaze so intently upon the closed door we don't see the window that's opened up ready to offer us a world of new possibilities. Keep your ears, heart, mind and soul open to a new beginning.

Avoid those who have the potential to rob your happiness and steal your sense of well-being.

"God helps those who help themselves," Benjamin Franklin once stated. What are you doing to help yourself today?

More than anything else, people will always remember you for how you made them feel. How you've managed to shine a light on their overcast moments. You never know how you can affect the life of another by your selfless actions. The feeling of hope that ripples and spreads joy never goes unnoticed.

Think and Be Happy

Keep yourself in the zone of happiness. This is not to say to completely ignore your duties and responsibilities. Simply take on a positive, healthy perspective of the situation and remain spiritually at peace even in the midst of chaos. Remember to only book one hour per week to worrying (since that's all the time it's worth) and postpone fretting over that problem until then—if you must. Spend the rest of your time in the Happy Zone by enjoying the precious time you have in life.

Having an entourage of empowering thoughts, cherished fond memories, and positive self-image are few of many principalities in the State of Happiness. Be sure to book your ticket and visit often.

You may wonder why some people are pleasant, calm and exude positive vibes towards others habitually even during troubling times. More than likely, they are under the influence of happiness brought on by the way they choose to think about their lives and their world, not merely the state of their lives or their world. This can be experienced and embraced by all of us.

Think and Be Happy

Many times, the formula for happiness has been revealed in various studies of habitually happy people. Some common denominators that often surface are those who know how to enjoy themselves, have a purpose, do satisfying work, make the most of challenges, don't dwell on the past, make it a point to relax, eat healthy, energize through exercise, live below their means, don't scrimp on sleep, they are adequately rested, do whatever brings them joy, and give joy to others among other things. These can act as powerful antidotes to being under the influence of stress.

When we find satisfaction in the work we do, find challenges and use them to top up our character's strength, do things that excite us, feel as if we have a purpose, cut out time spent on past recollections and live purposefully and joyfully in each moment, we experience the elixir for happiness.

Problems are great stimulators and motivators. They often drive us forward to solve situations and better ourselves in the process. They provide us challenges that our minds require to be active. Build brain power and character. There is a saying that states that a sailor becomes skilled not during the calm seas but by the stormy weather at sea. He best learns how to maneuver his way. Turbulent times can be blessings in disguise on our roads to happiness.

Have you had your dose of laughter today? Most habitually happy people have a laugh on a regular basis. Some, once a day. One of my fit, youthful looking, 87-year-old patients told me that she made sure to have steady diet of laughter injected into her daily routine. She would collect humorous videos and watch them or read a comic or recall a funny memory and have a good belly laugh. Laughter has been said to also have potentially healing qualities as endorphins, the body's "feel good" hormone, are released into the bloodstream. Where there is laughter, happiness is often close by.

Whatever we feel may be missing in our lives, not right, gone awry, whatever may be robbing us of joy in the moment, it is vital to know that *we* are equipped with the capacity and resources within to live the lives we desire by restructuring and redesigning our thoughts.

Make it a point to invite happiness into your home by sharing a chuckle and joy with those close to you, speaking and thinking optimistically, exercising forgiveness. Some homes are filled with despair and pain, but you can override this by infusing hope in any situation. When you bring laughter into your home, happiness follows.

When you decide to retire the thoughts that overwork your emotions, cause you to worry and drain your energy, you begin to truly live jubilantly in the moment as you experience happiness.

We all need a little push, a little drive, a little challenge, a little excitement, a little motivation from time to time. Never underestimate nor negate the hidden blessings in having problems or unfriendly naysayers. They can lift you to greatness if you set your mind to overcome and get through them armed with a positive mentality. Many well established, successful achievers have said similar words on the journey to excellence. That those who tried to belittle them, put them down, and told them they can't do it, have given them the motivation to prove their critics wrong and succeed against the odds. Malcolm X once said, "If you have no critics, you'll likely have no success."

Don't eat crap! It may seem a little harsh and unrefined in the spiritual advice arena, but the fact is that many of us not only listen to negativity but we accept the serving given to us by others. What's worse, we tend to take double servings and triple helpings by continuing to replay the negative scenario over in our minds thus eating into our peace and enjoyment-of-life time. Refuse and toss out negative thoughts and move forward to a more fulfilling experience.

Feelings of happiness begin with thoughts of happiness. What are you thinking right now? If you don't like what's playing in your mind—change it.

Create a jubilant journal. Fill in funny moments or times that bring a smile to your face or an upward curve to your lips. Like jewels, they are priceless at a later date. Retrieve and re-read these entries later to uplift your spirit. It could be a hilarious scene from a movie or favorite comedy clip. Keep a scrap book or retain happy moments to cherish later. Experience delight beyond your wildest imagination.

We all want to travel to the state of happiness but yet we forget that we need to bring only one piece of baggage. The present. Not the past nor the future. Live in the golden moment of now unaccompanied by concerns or cares.

Democritus said it well: "Happiness resides not in possessions and not in gold, the feeling of happiness dwells in the soul."

Ensure you keep yourself active doing positive activities that stimulate you and give you satisfaction. George Matthew Allen once said: "People with many interests live, not only longest, but happiest."

Take the time to appreciate the little things in life, as the old saying goes to "stop and smell the roses." Too many times we get so caught up in moving forward we forget to appreciate where we are and what we have.

Do whatever brings you joy and peace and satisfaction and purpose. Raising your children, hobbies, work, entertaining. Aldous Huxley once said, "Happiness is not achieved by the conscious pursuit of happiness; it is generally the by-product of other activities."

Remember this, if you remember nothing else, this statement by David Burns: "There is only one person who could ever make you happy, and that person is you!"

From the beginning of time, philosophers have reiterated over and over the importance eliminating worry as a requirement to happiness. Epictetus stated: "There is only one way to happiness, and that is to cease worrying about things which are beyond the power of our will."

Give of yourself sincerely. Engage in activities that bring you joy, make yourself useful. Give of your talents to help others. Share your gift with the world. Robert F. Kennedy once said, "You're happiest while you're making the greatest contribution."

Think and Be Happy

Take it slow. Savor each stage in your dream plan. Relax. Chew your food slowly and deliberately. Spend quality time conversing with a loved one. Perform a lengthy and rewarding task with your child. Don't race your thoughts ahead to what has to be done next but settle in the moment on the task you have at hand. As Mahatma Gandhi once said, "There is more to life than increasing its speed."

Think and Be Happy

Who cares what the next person thinks about you?! Frankly, it is none of your business what goes on in someone else's head. Do your best, feel your best and let your actions speak for themselves. Sometimes you can give everything you've got and there will be naysayers who will think whatever they will. Be more concerned with integrity, speaking up when it's necessary and being your best and feeling your best in your life. French philosopher Albert Camus once stated, "To be happy, we must not be too concerned with others."

Practice looking forward to possibilities. Look ahead to things getting better. Look forward to hope. Look forward to moving forward in your career. Look forward for your situation to get better eventually. Roman philosopher George Santayana once wrote, "Knowledge of what is possible is the beginning of happiness."

It all begins in the mentality. If you don't think you'll ever be happy, you probably will not experience the euphoric feeling of happiness. Publilius Syrus, 1st Century B.C. Latin philosopher, once stated, "No man is happy who does not think himself so."

Think and Be Happy

Happiness is vital to your mental health and sense of well-being. Exercise your right to be happy every day.

Think and Be Happy

What makes one person happy, may not make another happy. And that's okay. It's great to have similar interests with friends and family, but once you accept that, for instance, your spouse may love Sunday night football, your daughter may enjoy listening to her iPod or playing the piano, or your best friend may prefer comedy to romance, we can enrich our own lives by respecting our own tastes as well as those close to us. As English cleric Charles Caleb Colton once wrote: "Our minds are as different as our faces: we are all traveling to one destination—happiness; but few are going by the same road."

Forgive others but never forget to forgive yourself as well. Guilt makes for a terrible stay-up-nights stimulant. A clear mind, conscious and ego create a natural sedative and softer pillow to lay your mind to rest soundly at night. "How unhappy is he who cannot forgive himself," Latin philosopher Publilius Syrus once proclaimed.

When you believe with your heart and soul that good things are not only possible but they are coming your way, you open up the universal pathway for goodness to happen to you. As the book of Mark 9: 23 in the Holy Bible states: "All things are possible to him that believes."

It doesn't matter what your situation is or your ailment. You can still enjoy a healthy, happy existence. According to the World Health Organization, *Health* is generally defined as being in "a state of complete physical, mental, and social well-being and not merely the absence of disease or infirmity."

Make it your goal to have a good time in all that you do. This is a popular trait in habitually happy people according to research on the topic of what makes a person happy.

Develop the happiness habit and kick the old worry routine out the window. When you view situations with optimism, you not only have a brighter outlook on life but you experience a complete state of joy.

If you've ever experienced the euphoric feeling of being on cloud nine, make it a point to capture that moment and replay it often. Revisit the pleasant experience in your mind and relive the feelings of pure contentment.

Take the driver's seat every time when you feel as if your feelings are spinning out of control into the danger zone. Never let a situation or person take hold of your emotions. Don't divert off the road to happiness into the ditch of frustration. Seize the wheel and drive yourself independently, emotionally to where you want to be—your state of happiness and peace of mind.

There is great benefit in starting off your morning on a positive note. Empowering thoughts have the potential to richly bless your experiences throughout the day.

Think and Be Happy

It has been said that "Peace is not the absence of conflict, but the presence of God no matter what the conflict." Be at peace within.

Make a list of everything that makes you feel unhappy or overwhelmed. Next, do everything in your power to avoid those items as you mentally toss the idea of them out of your mind.

Practice living in the serenity of the moment. Practice. Practice. Practice. Never stop practicing. If you feel yourself slipping in your practice, get back into shape and sharpen those peace and happiness skills until it becomes second nature. Truly, practice makes perfect.

Think and Be Happy

The true source of your happiness will always be found in one place—within you.

Be you. And only you. Just as no two fingerprints are identical, as are no two minds, two souls or two hearts. Be proud of the unique design God has crafted you to be. And appreciate the uniquity of others, too, in order to enjoy harmonious relationships.

Don't let anyone fool you, happiness is not only your right, but it is what you make it to be.

.

We're all students in the course of life. Don't be ashamed of making mistakes. It's the only way we'll learn, grow and develop. The only way. Never stop learning and growing.

Take with you servings of hope and encouragement on your happiness diet. With supreme confidence, refuse to accept a plate of defeat or a side dish of negativity from others. Just say, "No, thank you." Be careful what you feed your mind and ultimately your soul on your journey to inner-peace and contentment.

You can safely call off your search for happiness today because the secret to where it lies has been revealed. It isn't in your new car, newfound love, bigger home, updated wardrobe, successful weight-loss program, fabulous job or other material or status symbols. It's simply within your mind. "The secrets to happiness are in your head," wrote Stephen M. Pollan and Mark Levine in *It's All In Your Head: Thinking Your Way to Happiness.* The authors further state that "attitude, not action" and "ways you think not steps you take" are all key elements to true happiness.

Think and Be Happy

Bad news first: For each person who lives there is only one person who holds the key to true, everlasting happiness. Good news: For you that person will always be: You.

Studies have shown that people who hold faith in a higher being tend to lead happier lives. Hebrews 11:1 in the NLT version of the Holy Bible answers: "What is faith? It is the confident assurance that what we hope for is going to happen. It is the evidence of things we cannot see."

Focus on pleasant memories. Happy thoughts from the past bring happy feelings into the present.

Think and Be Happy

Always remember that happiness is not about the state of your condition. It's about the state of your mind regardless of your condition.

Think and Be Happy

Believe in yourself with all your might and strength and believe that you are just right the way you are. Believe you can grow and develop on your journey in life at your individual pace. Believe you deserve goodness in life. Believe you have the power to bring good things to you. Believe you can become more and never stop believing in yourself. Mathew 21:22 tells us that "If you believe, you will receive whatever you ask for in prayer."

Enjoy your moments, since life is, in fact, made up of multiple links called moments. Listen to your favorite tune as you do household chores, uplifting music, relaxing music. Download older, fun music from iTunes that you've always wanted to hear that takes you back to a special moment in time. Have fun in all that you do. Your life is so worth it.

Remember, if you're stuck in a situation, your world seems depressing, surrounded by negative people, the Happy Zone is never far because it is located in your own mind. Bring it forth with a boost of optimism.

It's okay to go through twists and turns on the road to happiness. It's okay to fall down emotionally as long as you get back up and traverse the road again.

Think and Be Happy

Happiness is intimately personal and we are all responsible for our own feelings of joy.

Happiness occurs in our own minds where we will always have access to it. Always commit this jewel of information to mind and you'll have one of life's greatest treasures.

No matter what difficult or discouraging situation you may find yourself in, focus on getting your mind out of the circumstance first. When you are determined to break free of negative happenings, your actions usually follow the path paved by your thoughts.

Think and Be Happy

If you want a vacation from your troubles, pack your problems off with a good, strong mental attitude.

Be the light you want to see in a situation if you see some glum faces. Why not try to brighten someone's day with a warm smile or a kind word? If someone is being negative, try to inject a little optimism into the situation. As an old Chinese proverb states: "Better to light a candle than to curse the darkness."

Peace brings serenity in the middle of calamity. It brings inner strength and greater confidence. It brings clarity and a steady flow of positive energy and ideas. Peace brings unconditional happiness. Take the simple advice granted by Genesis 43:23 in the Holy Bible, "Peace be with you."

Forgiveness is both peace and power to the forgiver. As Mahatma Gandhi once said: "The weak can never forgive. Forgiveness is the attribute of the strong." Are you strong enough to handle forgiveness? You'll be on the road to happiness when you forgive because you release the hurt and the pain.

Think and Be Happy

If you're not happy in a task you are doing, change it if it is feasible or possible. If not, try to find something pleasant in what you're doing. There will always be favorable and unfavorable aspects in all circumstances. It depends on the eyes or mind of the person viewing the situation. As Dale Carnegie once said: "People rarely succeed unless they have fun in what they are doing."

Someone once said that "if you find a way to be thankful for your troubles, they can become your blessings." Be grateful for the good and the bad. They both help us to appreciate life more and they keep us in touch with reality as well as in a state of balance.

Don't be timid about being confronted with a problem or difficult situation. Successful people view it as nothing more than a challenge, a hurdle to be jumped over to something better. The wisdom of Einstein, one of the greatest minds of our time stated it well, "In the midst of difficulty lies opportunity."

Think and Be Happy

Follow Einstein's simple formula when you are on the road to happiness: "Learn from yesterday, live for today and hope for tomorrow."

Quite a lot of people forward this popular e-mail Irish Blessing to cheer up their friends and co-workers. Some keep it posted in their homes:

> *May your days be many and your troubles be few.*
> *May all God's blessings descend upon you.*
> *May peace be within you may your heart be strong.*
> *May you find what you're seeking wherever you roam.*

There is always an opportunity to be better, do better, think better, and to make others feel better. Be a well-wisher to strangers, too. When we are genuinely nice to others, the flow of goodness travels back to us. As Mother Teresa once said: "It is not the magnitude of our actions but the amount of love that is put into them that matters."

Life consists of precious moments. As an unknown author once stated: "Life is not measured by the number of breaths we take but by the number of moments that take our breath away."

Many happy people I've met seem to have a source of comfort. A passage in the Bible is treasured by many as one of the greatest sources. Following is the 23rd Psalm. Though the King James version is most quoted, here is a version from the New Living Translation Bible:

> *The Lord is my shepherd;*
> *I have all that I need.*
> *He lets me rest in green meadows;*
> *He leads me beside peaceful streams.*
> *He renews my strength.*
> *He guides me along right paths, bringing honor to*
> *his name.*
> *Even when I walk through the darkest valley,*
> *I will not be afraid, for You are close beside me.*
> *Your rod and Your staff protect and comfort me.*
> *You prepare a feast for me in the presence of my*
> *enemies.*
> *You honor me by anointing my head with oil.*
> *My cup overflows with blessings.*
> *Surely Your goodness and unfailing love will pursue*
> *me all the days of my life,*
> *and I will live in the house of the Lord forever.*

Amen